USING YOUR DECCA

By the same authors

Competent Crew: Second Edition
ISBN 0 7136 3421 9

Day Skipper: Second Edition
ISBN 0 7136 3422 7

VHF Yachtmaster
ISBN 0 229 11720 1

Yachtmaster: An Examination
Handbook with Exercises
(Revised and updated)
ISBN 0 7136 3521 5

Yachtmaster Exercises (Revised)
ISBN 0 229 11715 5

Ocean Yachtmaster: Celestial
Navigation – An Instructional
Handbook with Exercises
(Revised and updated)
ISBN 0 7136 3596 7

Ocean Yachtmaster Exercises:
Exercises in Celestial Navigation
ISBN 0 229 11792 9

Other titles of interest

How to Use Radar
by H G Strepp
ISBN 0 7136 3324 7

Using Loran
by Conrad Dixon
ISBN 0 7136 3567 3

USING YOUR DECCA

Pat Langley-Price and
Philip Ouvry

ADLARD COLES NAUTICAL
London

Published by Adlard Coles Nautical
an imprint of A & C Black (Publishers) Ltd
35 Bedford Row, London WC1R 4JH

First published in Great Britain by
Adlard Coles 1989
Reprinted 1990
Reprinted by Adlard Coles Nautical 1992

ISBN 0-7136-3597-5

A CIP catalogue record for this book is available
from the British Library.

Printed and bound in Great Britain by
Hartnolls Ltd, Bodmin, Cornwall

Acknowledgements

NAVSTAR SA
Shipmate Marine Electronics
AMPRO Distribution (for AP Navigator)
NASA Marine Electronics
Racal Marine
Stephen Lacey

Contents

List of figures

List of plates

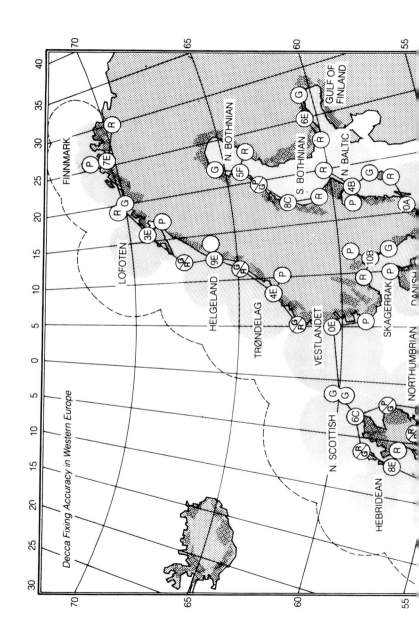

Decca Fixing Accuracy in Western Europe

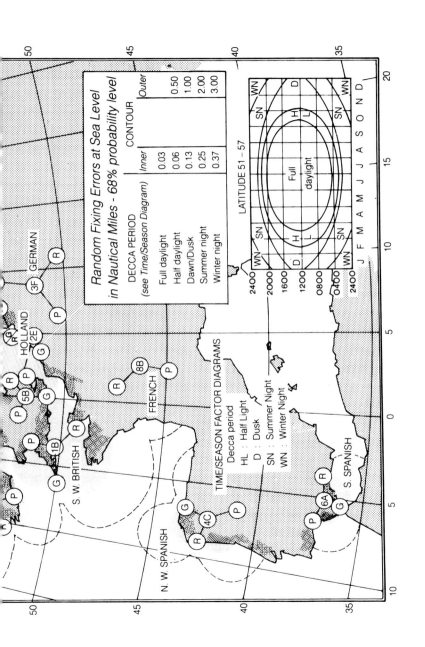

Random Fixing Errors at Sea Level in Nautical Miles - 68% probability level

DECCA PERIOD (see Time/Season Diagram)	CONTOUR	
	Inner	Outer
Full daylight	0.03	0.50
Half daylight	0.06	1.00
Dawn/Dusk	0.13	2.00
Summer night	0.25	2.00
Winter night	0.37	3.00

LATITUDE 51 – 57

TIME/SEASON FACTOR DIAGRAMS

Decca period
HL : Half Light
D : Dusk
SN : Summer Night
WN : Winter Night

GERMAN

HOLLAND

FRENCH

S. W. BRITISH

N. W. SPANISH

S. SPANISH

Introduction

Close on 72,000 small craft, motor and sailing, make passages along the coast or offshore in the seas surrounding the United Kingdom. In time nearly half these craft will be using an electronic navigation aid; and the most common of these will be the Decca Navigator system.

The Decca Navigator receivers used on these small craft are no longer manufactured by the Decca Navigator Company (which has become Racal Marine) but are manufactured by companies such as AP Navigator (Denmark), Shipmate Marine Electronics, Navstar SA, and NASA Marine Electronics. Kelvin Hughes, Vigil, Thomas Walker and LEAB (Sweden) have also produced Decca receivers. The Decca Yacht Navigator Mks 2, 3, and 4 were only marketed but not manufactured by the Decca Navigator Company. Some of these companies manufacture more than one version. So there are quite a number of different receivers available for small craft; and many of them appear to be very different from each other.

The Decca Navigator system uses radio signals to determine position. This type of system, which is known as a hyperbolic navigation system, uses groups of transmitters, called *chains*, positioned around north-west Europe. The radio waves (at medium frequencies) are detected by the shipborne receivers, which can then determine the vessel's position. In essence, that is all the shipborne receiver does: it determines the ship's present position. However, by using simple computing techniques, much other useful navigational information can be worked out, such as: course; speed; course to steer to the next point on a passage (a *waypoint*); the range and bearing of a waypoint; and the time it will take to reach it at present speed. These extra facilities give rise to the large number of buttons on the Decca receiver; initially there was a separate button for each function but on modern receivers a combination or sequence of buttons is pressed to select particular functions.

More seafarers are installing electronic gadgets, and some can achieve remarkable results with them. Others may be confused by the range and versatility of the functions. The objective of this book is to simplify the mystique of these electronic aids to navigation so that they can be operated by all seafarers without recourse to any special training in either electronics or navigation.

It has been a little difficult to write this book so that it covers the wide variation in operating procedures of the different makes of Decca receiver. However the principles of navigation using the Decca Navigation system are the same no matter which make of Decca receiver is used. The **Navstar 2000D** has proved to be a very popular choice among owners of both sailing and motor boats, so most examples given in this book are based on the operating procedures for this receiver.

Seafarers contemplating long passages beyond the coastlines of north-west Europe should be aware of the limited geographical coverage of the Decca system. The **Loran-C** navigator system covers the Mediterranean Sea and the eastern seaboard of the United States so, in a sense, it complements the

Decca system coverage. However it will be the **Global Positioning System** (GPS) satellite navigator that will eventually give global coverage to the same degree of accuracy as the Decca and Loran-C. **Omega** is a low frequency hyperbolic radio navigation system with global coverage but with limited accuracy, and is thus suitable only for ocean navigation.

Though this book sets out to extol the simplicity of navigation at sea using the Decca Navigator system, it must be emphasised that it is an aid to navigation and is no substitute for knowledge of the theory of navigation and experience of putting the theory into practice. However, the presence on board of a Decca receiver will, we hope, give the erstwhile navigator the confidence to venture towards new horizons, thus appreciating the enjoyment of cruising to far-away places unfettered by the crowded timetables of modern transport services.

May we wish you many happy voyages.

Pat Langley-Price
Philip Ouvry

1 Navigate simply

The Decca Navigator receiver, which will be referred to throughout as 'Decca', as fitted on small craft, picks up radio waves from shorebased transmitters from which the boat's present position is determined. This position is normally displayed in coordinates of latitude and longitude. So to navigate with a Decca we must have: (a) a chart with a grid of latitude and longitude; (b) a compass rose or protractor for measuring direction on the chart; and (c) an instrument, such as dividers or a ruler, for measuring distance.

Whenever we mark the present position on a chart, normally shown as a dot with a circle round it ($\odot$) and known as a *fix*, it is very important to mark alongside it the time. From a series of fixes taken at regular intervals we can see the direction in which the boat is going (*course made good* or *track*), work out its speed achieved over the land (*speed made good*), and estimate the time of arrival (*ETA*) at the next point on the passage (*waypoint*).

However, most Deccas have their own simple computer which will work out the speed made good (*SMG*) and course made good (*CMG*); and, if we enter the coordinates (latitude and longitude) of the waypoints, it will work out from the boat's

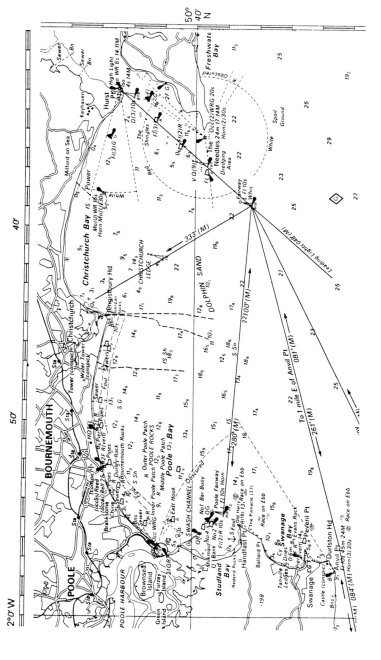

Fig 1.1 A small scale chart showing latitude and longitude

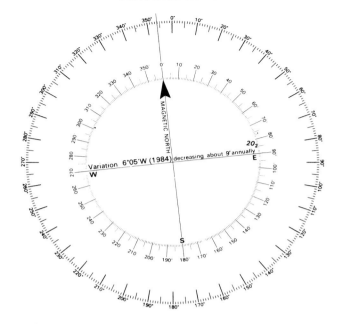

Fig 1.2 Compass rose

present position the distance (known as *range*) and direction (known as *bearing*) of the next waypoint and estimate the time it will take to reach it. So we can now navigate very simply by using the coordinates from the Decca to determine our position on the chart (either by latitude and longitude or by the range and bearing from a charted landmark) and by using the chart to enter the coordinates of our next waypoint into the Decca. Yes – there are other factors involved with navigation and there is no substitute for experience and formal training, but the Decca gives us the means of knowing at all times our present position and of working out the direction to steer to reach our destination.

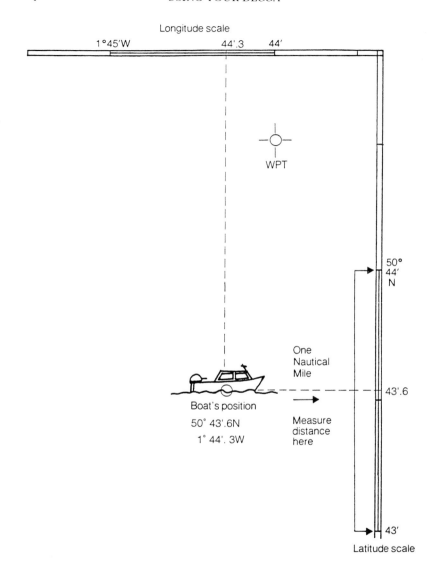

Fig 1.3   Measuring coordinates of latitude and longitude. Always measure distance on the latitude scale level with boat's position

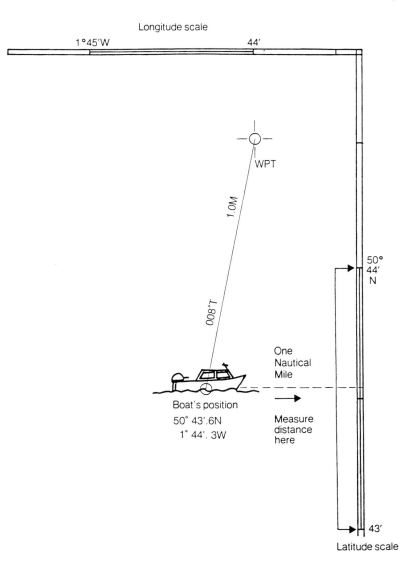

Fig 1.4   Measuring the bearing and range of a waypoint (WPT 2)

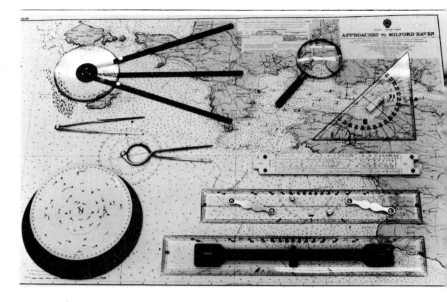

Plate 1   Various plotting instruments

2 Starting up (Initialisation)

Throughout the book the operational sequences appropriate to the NAVSTAR 2000D will be used. For other Decca receivers the operator's manual should be consulted, though the principles of operation are the same for all receivers.

The initial switching on and setting up of the Decca is normally referred to as *initialisation*. Once switched on the Decca is designed to operate continuously throughout a passage, so the ON/OFF switch is frequently at the side (or even at the back) of the Decca unit. Once switched on the Decca will carry out a series of self-checks and the display will illuminate.

The Decca requires some basic information before it can operate effectively. This information includes the date and time, the initial position, the chart datum and the magnetic variation.

The Decca has a memory (operated by an internal rechargeable battery) which retains previously entered information, including the coordinates of the position at the time it was last switched off, so much of the initialisation sequence only requires the acceptance of data retained in the memory. The date and time will need to be entered each time the Decca is switched on. Details of the method of data entry are explained later in this chapter.

The Decca receives radio signals from a *chain* of transmitters consisting of a master and three (though sometimes only two) slave transmitters. As explained in Chapter 14 a master/slave combination will provide one *line of position*. Two lines of position are needed to determine position, and a third is desirable. The Decca cannot determine position until it receives at least two pairs of signals. When it is receiving enough signals to determine position it is said to be 'locked on' and the *lock* light will illuminate. The status of the signal acquisition process (CHAIN SEARCH, SIGNAL FOUND, CHECKING POSITION, SYSTEM READY) can be checked by pressing the status key $\boxed{STA}$ once. Press the $\boxed{STA}$ key again to determine the received signal strength. On a scale increasing from 1 to 9 the master (M) should be at least 8 and the slaves (R – *red*, G – *green*, P – *purple*) should be at least 7. Pressing the $\boxed{STA}$ key a third time will give a figure indicating the overall reception quality.

If the boat has not been moved since the Decca was switched off, it can lock on immediately using the position retained in its memory. If the boat, or the Decca receiver, has been moved then it will be necessary to enter the coordinates (latitude and longitude) of the present position as part of the initialisation. If the lock light does not illuminate, then the latitude and longitude indicated may not represent the present position. For the NAVSTAR 2000D the position entered must be correct to within 3 nautical miles of the actual position. The AP MK4 and MK5 can work out the actual position with no input position (though it may take 20 minutes).

DATA ENTRY

Note: The method of data entry can vary considerably,

depending on the type of Decca receiver. The Owner's or Operator's Manual must be referred to for details.

Position

When entering positions, note the following points:

1. First latitude and then longitude are entered by pressing the appropriate number keys (known as *punching in*) with degrees and minutes in succession and using the decimal point (.) to separate tenths of a minute. The ⊹ or +/− key is the interchange key used to change north (N) to south (S) and east (E) to west (W) when entering positions in latitude and longitude. It is important to remember to enter two digits when entering minutes: do not suppress the leading zero.

For example:

Latitude 7° 20'.1N would be entered:

7 2 0 . 1 ENT and displayed

LAT
N 7.20.10

and 35° 7'.12S would be entered:

3 5 0 7 . 1 2 +/- ENT and displayed

LAT
S 35.07.12

Longitude 153° 01'.7W would be entered:

1 5 3 0 1 . 7 +/- ENT and displayed

LONG
W 153.01.70

and 1° 59'.9E would be entered:

1 5 9 . 9 ENT and displayed

LONG
E   1.59.90

2. It is necessary to move the display between functions either by repeated pressing of the function selection key ([PRG] for NAVSTAR) or the roll key [R↑]. This procedure is known as *rolling* the display. Having entered the latitude the display is rolled to show longitude and, once the longitude has been entered, rolled again to the next function in the same group.

3. Incorrect inputs can be changed by pressing the [ENT] key again and entering the correct data. In some Deccas the display will alternate between bright and dim to indicate that it is expecting an input. If the data is already in memory it will be shown as a dim display which can be accepted by pressing the [ENT] key or overwritten with fresh data. The accepted data is shown as a bright display. Data shown in a dim display will be accepted if the display is rolled.

Time and Date

The initialisation sequence frequently requests the input of time and date to be entered in a similar manner to latitude and longitude.

For example:

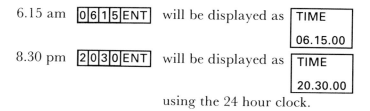

6.15 am [0][6][1][5][ENT] will be displayed as
```
TIME

06.15.00
```

8.30 pm [2][0][3][0][ENT] will be displayed as
```
TIME

20.30.00
```
using the 24 hour clock.

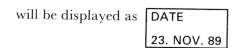

23rd November 1989 [2][3][1][1][8][9][ENT]

will be displayed as
```
DATE

23. NOV. 89
```

4th January 1990 | 0 | 4 | 0 | 1 | 9 | 0 | ENT |

will be displayed as | DATE |
| 04. JAN. 90 |

Time and date are not necessary for navigation, but are used for recording the date and time (*datetime*) of last fix, of man overboard, or when an alarm function is initiated.

Datum

The chart datum is entered after installation and afterwards only when entering a new geographical area. The alternative chart datums available are: UK, Eire, Europe, Canada, South Africa, Australia, Japan, India, Persian Gulf and WGS 72. WGS 72 is a world geographical scale datum and may be used if no other datums are suitable.

For NAVSTAR 2000D press the | PRG | key and then press the [◆] key until the appropriate chart datum is displayed.

| DATUM |
| UK |

Chain

All Decca receivers, with the exception of the NASA D200A will automatically select the nearest group of transmitters (known as a *chain*) during initialisation.

When in a region approximately equidistant between two chains, the Decca, when in the automatic chain selection mode, may dither between the two sets of signals causing an alarm condition with the indication NEAR NEW CHAIN or SWITCHED CHAIN. In these conditions it may be prudent to select manually one chain until the boat is clear of the region of interaction. For NAVSTAR 2000D the [◆] key is used in conjunction with the

$\boxed{\text{CHN}}$ key to switch from automatic to manual chain selection. The number keys are used to select letters by substitution of the letters A to I for the numbers 1 to 9.

For example:

North British Chain number 3B

$\boxed{3}\boxed{2}\boxed{\text{ENT}}$ would be displayed as $\boxed{\begin{array}{l}\text{MANUAL} \\ \text{CHAIN 3B}\end{array}}$

The Decca chain numbers for north west Europe are shown on pp. x and xi, and are listed in all Decca operator's manuals.

Most Decca receivers can operate in a separate Dead Reckoning (DR) mode, in which the computing capability is used independent of any Decca system signals to estimate navigational outputs (course made good, speed made good, time to waypoint, etc.).

3   Position

The POSITION function is normally selected by pressing the key
marked [POS]. For normal operation, when the POSITION
function has been selected and the Decca signal strength is
sufficient to achieve lock (*lock* light illuminated), the display
will indicate the latitude (LAT) and longitude (LONG) of the
present position. For example:

```
N 50.23.03

W 1.54.71
```

Note that the LAT and LONG are displayed to the nearest
hundredth of a minute: this is a function of the display rather
than a measure of the accuracy of the receiver (see Chapter 11).

If LOCK has been lost or there is some reason why the Decca
is doubtful about the accuracy of the position, then this will be
indicated on the display as an alarm condition and the *lock* light
may be extinguished. The alarm conditions may be: NEAR
WAYPOINT, NEAR NEW CHAIN, SWITCHED CHAIN, POSITION SUS-
PECT, SIGNAL SUSPECT, INVALID PATTERN, SIGNAL LOST or
ANTENNA FAIL.

If the Decca detects a discrepancy of more than 0.5 nautical miles between the three lines of position obtained from a Decca chain, then the *lock* light will flash. If the *lock* light is extinguished *all display data must be ignored*.

If the Decca has lost lock and the present position can be determined by another means (such as visual bearings of navigation marks), the Decca present position can be updated. For NAVSTAR 2000D this is achieved by reverting to the initialisation mode by pressing the PRG button five times and entering the actual position. Note that the input position should be correct to within 3 nautical miles and that it can take up to 4 minutes for the Decca to LOCK on. (**NB** A nautical mile is not the same as a statute mile. It is equivalent to one minute as measured on the latitude scale and is approximately 2,000 yards, or 1,852 metres. Hence, the latitude scale on a chart is used for measuring distance. The longitude scale is not the same as the latitude scale and must not be used for distance measurements.)

It is the general rule to leave the Decca switched to display the present position. For passages lasting over a period of several hours, it is good navigational practice to keep a record of the present position at regular intervals (on a chart or in a journal called the *deck log*) so that if there is a problem with the Decca it is readily evident when the problem occurred and an estimate of position may be made, based on the boat's course and speed.

4 Velocity

COURSE AND SPEED MADE GOOD

The VELOCITY function is normally selected by a push button marked VEL. When this function is selected, the boat's speed and course *over the land* are displayed. This speed over the land is known as the *speed made good* (SMG) and the course as the *course made good* (CMG) or *track*. Speed made good and course made good should not be confused with boat's speed and course as indicated by the speed log and compass, as these instruments do not take account of tidal stream or of any tendency of the wind to push the boat sideways (leeway).

SMG and CMG are derived from a series of positions averaged over a time period. This time period is normally 4 minutes, so the SMG and CMG displayed will only be accurate provided the boat has been on a steady course and speed for at least 4 minutes.

By rolling the display after the VELOCITY function VEL has been selected (in NAVSTAR 2000D press VEL a second time), the tidal stream direction and rate can be entered.

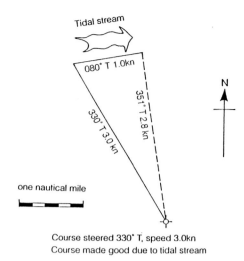

Tidal stream

080° T 1.0kn

351° T 2.8 kn

330° T 3.0 kn

one nautical mile

N

Course steered 330° T, speed 3.0kn
Course made good due to tidal stream

Fig 4.1   Speed and course made good

TIDAL STREAM

Details of tidal streams, which are changing continuously, are obtained either direct from a chart or from a tidal stream atlas. For hourly intervals they are shown as a direction (towards which the tidal stream is flowing) and a rate in knots (nautical miles per hour); see Figs 4.2 and 4.3

This data would need to be updated every hour so has only a limited use in passage making. The data is entered by punching in the appropriate figures and then pressing the ENTER ENT button. Pressing the ENT button a second time enables corrections to be made. Note that all directions are given in three-figure notation.

For example, a tidal stream of 045° 1.8 knots would be entered:

⬦W⬦	Hours	Dir	Rate Sp	Np
Before HW	3	206°	2.8	1.5
	2	207°	1.6	0.8
	1	053°	0.4	0.2
After HW	HW	040°	1.8	1.0
	1	035°	2.3	1.3

The tidal stream sets towards the direction shown. The rate is in knots.

A portion of a table from a chart, typically showing the tidal stream at the position on the chart indicated by the symbol ⬦w⬦. The time (Hours) refers to the time of High Water (HW) at the reference port shown above the table on the chart. The time at which the tidal stream data is required is entered in the table as an interval before or after HW. The direction and rate of the tidal stream can then be extracted. The rate is dependent on whether the tides are springs (Sp) or neaps (Np).

Fig 4.2   Tidal streams: tidal diamonds

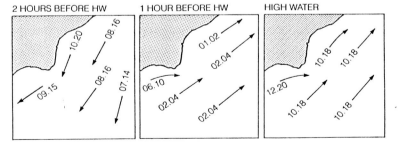

Fig 4.3   Tidal streams: tidal stream atlas

⊙4⊙5⊙ENT which would be displayed as ┌─────────┐
                                        │ TIDE DIR │
                                        │   045T   │
                                        └─────────┘

⊙1⊙.⊙8⊙ENT which would be displayed as ┌─────────┐
                                         │ TIDE SPD │
                                         │ 1.8 KN │
                                         └─────────┘

In the NAVSTAR 2000D the display alternates between tidal direction and tidal rate.

COMPASS VARIATION

In some Deccas the *compass variation* can be entered by further rolling of the ⊙VEL function. For NAVSTAR 2000D it is entered as part of the initialisation procedure. Compass variation at any geographical position is defined as the difference in direction of the geographical north pole and the magnetic north pole. Variation changes with geographical position and also very gradually with time. Variation for an area is shown on the *compass rose* on a chart; see Fig 1.2. The changes in variation which occur as one passes round the coast of Europe are small and would not affect a passage of under 200 nautical miles.

For example:

A variation of 5° 20′W would be entered:

⊙5⊙2⊙0⊙+/–⊙ENT and displayed as ┌──────────┐
                                   │ MAG - VAR │
                                   │ Y   05.20W │
                                   └──────────┘

The ⊙ or ⊙+/–⊙ button is used to switch the display to west variation.

(For NAVSTAR 2000D the Y shows that magnetic variation will be applied to all displays of bearing, course made good and course to steer.)

5 Waypoints

WAYPOINTS are positions of which the latitude and longitude can be stored in the Decca's memory. Generally up to nine such positions can be stored, but in some Deccas up to two hundred can be stored.

WAYPOINT ENTRY

Selecting the WAYPOINT function (for NAVSTAR 2000D press the WPT key once, or, in other Deccas, roll the display R↑ as appropriate to select the Waypoint Entry mode) enables a

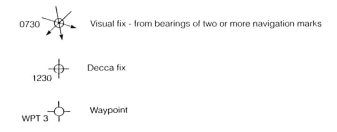

Fig 5.1   Symbols for plotting position

waypoint to be entered into the memory. First the WAYPOINT NUMBER is entered, and then its latitude and longitude.

For example:

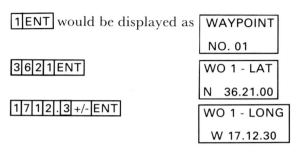

WAYPOINT RANGE, BEARING AND COURSE TO STEER

When the WAYPOINT [WPT] is pressed twice, the WAYPOINT NUMBER is entered. The display will then indicate the range, bearing and course to steer for that waypoint.

For example:

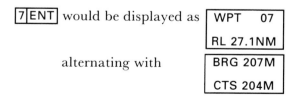

The COURSE TO STEER can be displayed either as a true course or as a magnetic (**M**) or compass (**C**) course, depending on whether variation and deviation have been previously entered. If any TIDAL STREAM has been entered (see Chapter 4), then the COURSE TO STEER allows for tidal stream. (*Note* RL in the display stands for a Rhumb Line course, which is normal for passages of less than 200 nautical miles. GC is used for longer passages in Great Circle navigation.)

WAYPOINT CROSS TRACK ERROR

When the WAYPOINT $\boxed{\text{WPT}}$ key is pressed a third time, the Waypoint Cross Track Error is displayed. For example:

$$\boxed{\begin{array}{l} \text{TO TRACK} \\ \text{<< 4.20NM} \end{array}}$$

The *cross track error* is the distance off course in nautical miles from the ideal track between the previously selected waypoints, or between the initialisation position and the selected waypoint. The method of its calculation and presentation varies from one type of Decca to another. There is usually an indication to the helmsman (<< or >> or alternatively ᒻ or ᒪ) to show which way to steer the boat back to the ideal course. In NAVSTAR 2000D the cross track error can be reset at any time by pressing $\boxed{\text{0}}\boxed{\text{ENT}}$.

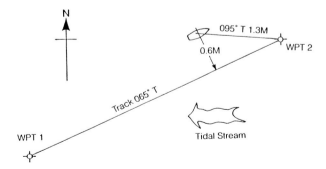

Fig 5.2   Cross Track Error – the vessel is 0.6 nautical miles off track to port. The helmsman will need to turn to starboard to return to track

If the Decca has the facility to store a sequence of waypoints representing the *sailplan* of a passage, then the COURSE TO STEER and CROSS TRACK ERROR will change automatically as the *closest point of approach* (CPA) is reached. The Decca detects the moment at which the range of the waypoint starts to increase and takes this moment to be the CPA.

ESTIMATED TIME TO WAYPOINT

When the WAYPOINT $\boxed{\text{WPT}}$ key is pressed a fourth time the *estimated time to waypoint* (in hours and minutes) will be displayed. For example:

$$\boxed{\begin{array}{l}\text{TIME TO}\\ \text{GO 1.42}\end{array}}$$

The estimated time to waypoint is calculated from the present position based on the speed made good (SMG) averaged over the previous 4 minutes. The time displayed can vary considerably if the SMG is changing so should normally be used only if the boat has been on a steady course and speed for ten minutes or so. Some Deccas will also indicate the *estimated time of arrival* (ETA), which is the clock time of arrival at the selected waypoint.

SAILPLAN ENTRY

The use of waypoints for sailplans and in passage planning is discussed in Chapter 7. A *sailplan* or *route* consists of a series of pre-programmed waypoints arranged in the order to be used. Typically a Decca may accept 9 sailplans, each containing 25 waypoints. Not all Deccas have a sailplan facility and, as

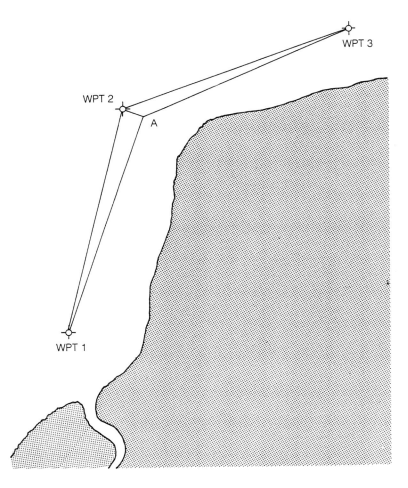

Fig 5.3   Closest Point of Approach (CPA). Point A represents the closest
point of approach to WPT 2

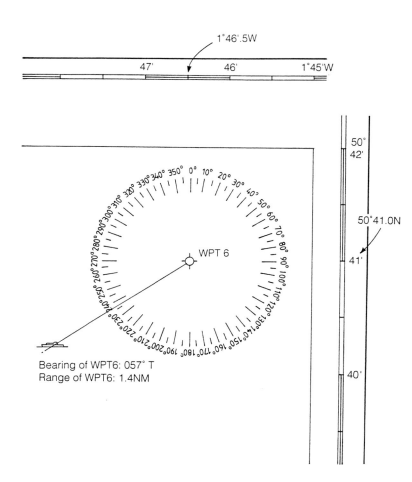

Fig 5.4   Using a compass rose as a waypoint centre. The coordinates of
WPT 6 are entered as 50°41'.0N 1°46'.5W, corresponding to the
centre of the compass rose. At any time the range and bearing of
WPT 6 can be easily plotted on the chart without the need to use
the latitude and longitude scales

method of entry varies considerably, the appropriate operator's manual should be used for reference. Some Deccas can be taken ashore, where the sailplans can be entered at home.

WAYPOINT CENTRE

To avoid having to plot on the chart the latitude and longitude of the present position at regular intervals, some navigators use the centre point of one of the compass roses marked on the chart as a *waypoint centre*. It is then relatively easy to plot the boat's range and bearing from the waypoint centre.

6   Control/test

The majority of Decca receivers have certain control and test functions, which are either selected directly or by rolling $\boxed{\text{R}\uparrow}$ from a master control function. The control functions include:

SELF TEST ROUTINE

The Self Test Routine is normally carried out as part of the initialisation procedure. If FAIL is displayed, then check all connections and try again. If FAIL appears persistently, then the Decca will have to be returned to the dealer.

DISPLAY BRIGHT/DIM

The display, normally bright, can be dimmed for night use.

SIGNAL QUALITY

The signal quality is normally displayed for the master (M) and the three slave (R – red, G – green, P – purple) transmitters in the selected chain. The quality is shown on an increasing scale from 1 (poor) to 9 (good). For satisfactory reception the quality figures should be not less than M8, R7, G7, P7.

For NAVSTAR 2000D Press the STATUS $\boxed{\text{STA}}$ key twice to display quality of reception.

```
SIG M9
R9 G9 P9
```

STRENGTH OF SIGNAL RECEPTION

Some Deccas will display overall signal strength as a single number. This number is only valid for comparative purposes but it is useful as a monitor of changes in receiver sensitivity at different times of the day and in different seasons. Radio propagation is best at midday in summer and worst at midnight in winter.

MANUAL CHAIN SELECTION

Particularly in a region equidistant between two chains, it is occasionally desirable to select manually (rather than automatically) the Decca chain to use. See Chapter 2.

ALARMS

Alarm condition will be displayed visually (and audibly if

selected) for the following reasons: NEAR WAYPOINT, NEAR NEW CHAIN, SWITCHED CHAIN, POSITION SUSPECT, INVALID PATTERN, SIGNAL LOST, ANTENNA FAIL. If the lock light goes out then all data displayed must be ignored. Alarms related to signal reception may indicate a temporary situation: displayed positions and other data during such conditions must be treated with caution. If the signal reception has been poor over a period of one hour or more, when the signal strength recovers the Decca receiver may have ambiguous information on the identification of the Decca 'lane' which will be indicated by flashing of the lock light, together with a Lane Identity (LI) alarm. Whilst the displayed position may be right, it should be treated with suspicion and cross-checked with a visual fix at the earliest opportunity. At that time it may be necessary to re-enter the actual position. Under these conditions it may be possible to confirm the actual position by manually selecting a more distant chain.

7 Waypoint selection

PRE-PLANNING

Before making a long passage it is worth making a list of the
appropriate waypoints. A series of permanent waypoints can
be selected and marked on the charts, bearing in mind the
following considerations:

1. The waypoint lies between the outer pair of buoys of a
   marked channel, e.g. in the Needles Channel between
   Bridge and SW Shingles.
2. The waypoint is in a harbour entrance, e.g. Braye Harbour
   in Alderney; or near (not at) a landfall buoy, e.g. Fairway off
   the Needles Channel.
3. The waypoint lies at the outer end of a transit line, e.g. the
   approach to St Peter Port, Guernsey, via the Little Russel
   Channel.
4. The waypoint lies at a safe distance from some headland or
   hidden danger, e.g. the end of St Albans Race.
5. The waypoint lies approximately in the route of an offshore
   passage and has simple coordinates. There should be

waypoints at regular intervals on the proposed passage. It is useful to mark waypoints at points on the passage where adjacent charts overlap.

For a passage that is likely to be repeated these waypoints can be marked permanently, with their coordinates written close by.

PLANNING

If the Decca has a *sailplan* facility then the waypoint sequence is entered. All waypoints entered should be recorded in the *deck log*. This waypoint entry can be done at any time; some navigators even take the receiver home to do it.

SETTING OFF

Before casting off, switch on the Decca and allow enough time for it to go through the initialisation procedure and lock on to the present position. In most receivers the switch-on position is the starting point of the first leg to the first waypoint, so any *cross track errors* during the navigation of a winding channel out of the harbour will have no significance. As the boat passes the first waypoint the receiver should automatically switch to the display for the second waypoint. If this facility is not available, then the second waypoint is selected manually.

As each waypoint is reached the time and distance log reading should be entered in the deck log. The Decca position should be plotted on the chart or entered in the deck log at regular intervals (30 minutes) so that, should the Decca fail, an estimate can be made of the present position and the courses and distance to the destination. (The Decca position can be

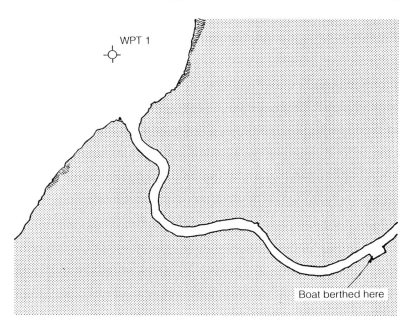

WPT 1

Boat berthed here

Fig 7.1   Winding channel

entered in the deck log either as a latitude and longitude or as a range and bearing to the next waypoint. The latter is normally much easier to plot.)

ALLOWANCE FOR TIDAL STREAM

As a waypoint is passed the bearing of the next waypoint can be displayed. If this course is steered for a few minutes a cross track error will begin to grow and the arrows will indicate an alteration of course to compensate for the cross track effect of the tidal stream. If the course made good (CMG) display is selected a comparison can be made with the course steered and an appropriate correction made to the course steered to counter the tidal stream. For instance, if the course steered is 260° (M) and the course made good is 265° (M), the course steered should be adjusted to 255° (M), which should cause the course made good to change to 260° (M) and the cross track error to reduce to zero.

As the tidal stream is not constant, this procedure has to be repeated at regular intervals (every hour). Some Deccas allow the tidal stream prediction for the next hour to be entered, which enables the course to steer to be calculated and displayed. The component of tidal stream along the course can be estimated by comparing the boat's speed (through the water) with the speed made good display.

LANDFALL AND APPROACH

Proper selection of waypoints should make the identification of navigational features and the location of the landfall or fairway buoy straightforward. In poor visibility be aware that other

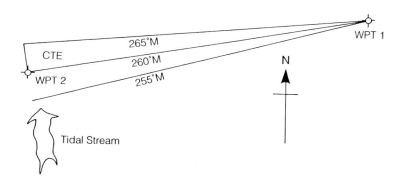

Fig 7.2   Reducing Cross Track Error (CTE)

vessels may well be using the same waypoint position so keep a good lookout. It is good practice to record in the deck log the exact Decca coordinates of key positions used in precise navigation (such as a harbour entrance). There may be positional errors in the Decca readings but they are usually constant so that it is possible to return to the same position with a high degree of confidence.

ARRIVAL

On arrival the sailplan and waypoints for the next leg of the passage are entered. If the destination is an anchorage, record the Decca coordinates of the position where the anchor is dropped. Some Deccas incorporate a waypoint alarm which can be set to sound off when the boat's position is a certain distance from a waypoint (which could be the anchor position). Thus, if the anchor drags the alarm will sound. In harbour the Decca is normally switched off.

8 Passage making

Let us plan a passage from Poole, on the south coast of England, to Cherbourg on the north coast of France and thence round Cape Barfleur to St Vaast-la-Hougue on the eastern side of the Cherbourg peninsula. We will make the passge using the Decca navigation system.

PLANNING

We must first obtain the relevant charts and sailing directions (pilots) and for these we need access to a nautical bookshop or chart agent. (Warsash Nautical Bookshop[1], Kelvin Hughes[2] and Kings of Lymington[3] operate a mail order service and supply a free catalogue.)

1. Warsash Nautical Bookshop, 31 Newtown Road, Warsash, Southampton, Hants SO3 6FY.
2. Kelvin Hughes Ltd., 145 Minories, London EC3N 1NH.
3. Kings of Lymington Bookshop, 105–6 High Street, Lymington, Hants SO4 0ZD.

If we use Admiralty charts, we will select (from the Home Waters catalogue NP 109) the following charts:

Chart No.	Title
2611	Poole Harbour and Approaches
2175	Poole Bay
2656	English Channel – Central Part
1106	Approaches to Cherbourg
2602	Cherbourg
2073	Pte de Barfleur to Courseulles
1349	Ports in Normandy

If we decide on Stanfords charts, which are published specially for yachtsmen, we would select charts 15 (Poole Harbour and Approaches) and 7 (English Channel – Solent to Cherbourg). The relevant Imray charts (which are also published for yachtsmen) are C4 (Needles to Portland Bill), C12 (Eastern English Channel) and C32 (Baie de Seine – Le Havre to Cherbourg).

For sailing directions we would select publications specially produced for yachtsmen, such as *Normandy and Channel Islands Pilot* by Mark Brackenbury (publisher Adlard Coles) or *Channel Harbours and Anchorages* by K. Adlard Coles (publisher Nautical). Closer examination of the sailing directions reveals that large scale plans of harbours and their approaches are included, which would then make it unnecessary to purchase (in this instance) Admiralty charts 2602 and 1349. Large scale Stanfords charts (published by Barnacle Marine) include sailing directions on the reverse but, for an unfamiliar passage, not in sufficient detail to make unnecessary the purchase of the local sailing directions. We also need a nautical almanac (e.g. *Reed's*, *Macmillan*, *Channel West & Solent*) for details of times of tides and tidal streams. These almanacs, published annually for yachtsmen, also include much more useful information, including coordinates of key waypoints.

Looking first at the small scale chart No. 2656 covering the central part of the English Channel, we can pick out the main components of the passage to prepare a sailplan (see examples below).

SAILPLAN NO. <u>1</u>

Waypoint List

ROUTE: Poole to Cherbourg

	DESCRIPTION	LAT	LONG	DIST (NM)	BRG (°True)
WP1	Poole Fairway Buoy	50° 39'.0N	1° 54'.8W	46.5	172
WP2	Edge of Chart 1106	49° 53'.0N	1° 44'.5W	9.8	172
WP3	CH1 buoy transit	49° 43'.3N	1° 42'.5W	3.6	141
WP4	Cherbourg W. ent.	49° 40'.5N	1° 39'.0W	1.7	121
WP5	Inner harbour ent.	49° 39'.6N	1° 36'.7W	0.6	198
WP6	Marina ent.	49° 39'.0N	1° 37'.0W	—	—
WP7					
WP8	} not used				
WP9					

Notes on Sailplans:

1. If a SAILPLAN or ROUTE function is available on the Decca, the waypoints have been set out in order of entry. In Sailplan 2, WPT5 is the same waypoint from Sailplan 1 so it does not have to be re-entered.

SAILPLAN NO. 2

Waypoint List

ROUTE: Cherbourg to St Vaast-la-Hougue

	DESCRIPTION	LAT	LONG	DIST (NM)	BRG (°True)
–	Marina ent.	—	—	0.6	018
WPT5	Inner harbour ent.	49°39'.6N	1°36'.7W	1.0	046
WPT1	Cherbourg E. ent.	49°40'.3W	1°35'.6W	5.5	052
WPT2	Raz W. card buoy	49°43'.7W	1°29'.0W	4.7	074
WPT3	N. card buoy	49°45'.0N	1°22'.0W	6.2	117
WPT4	off Pte de Barfleur	49°42'.2N	1°13'.5W	5.4	172
WPT6	off Dranguet E. card	49°36'.8N	1°12'.4W	2.5	198
WPT7	S. card buoy	49°34'.4N	1°13'.6W	0.6	270
WPT8	St Vaast Gde Rade	49°34'.4N	1°14'.6W	0.9	330
WPT9	St Vaast breakwater	49°35'.2N	1°15'.3W	—	—

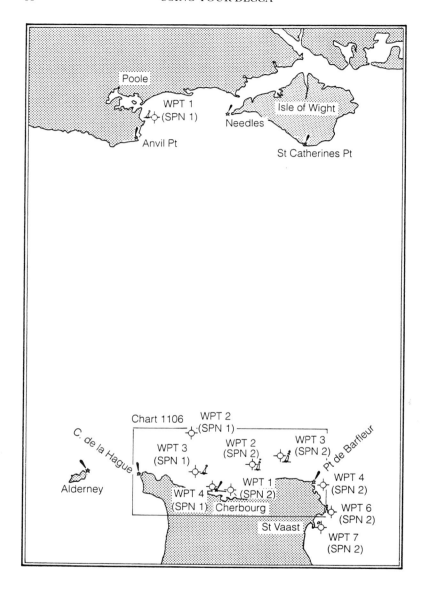

Fig 8.1   Waypoints for Sailplans 1 and 2 (SPN 1 and SPN 2)

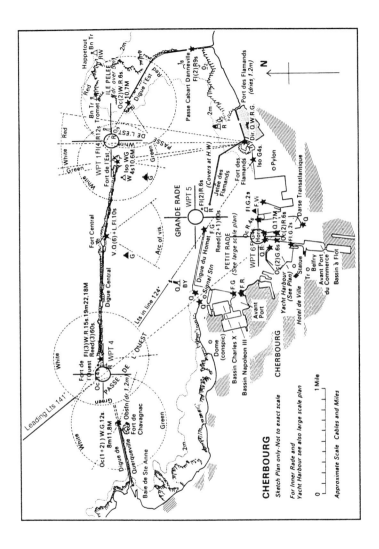

Fig 8.2 Detailed waypoints in Cherbourg

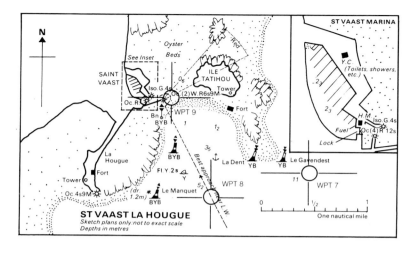

Fig 8.3   Detailed waypoints in St Vaast

2. It has been assumed that the Decca is limited to 9 waypoints. If more waypoints are available then they can be programmed in before the voyage commences and the sailplan amended accordingly.

3. To obtain the correct cross track error display, the Waypoint Cross Track Error will need to be reset at each waypoint (unless this is done automatically).

4. In Sailplan 1, WPT2 marks the point of change-over to the larger scale chart (No. 1106). It is always good practice to mark the waypoint on the change-over to another chart.

5. In Sailplan 1, waypoints WPT3 and WPT4 are on the transit of the leading lights into Cherbourg harbour. This transit is not visible by day.

6. If compass variation has been entered, then all bearings will be magnetic.

DEPARTURE

Before departure the Decca is switched on and the initialisation
sequence completed. The departure from Poole Town quay to
Poole harbour entrance is straightforward pilotage, and the
Decca is of little assistance. Again, the buoyed channel from the
harbour entrance to Poole Fairway buoy is straightforward,
but the Decca will indicate the range and bearing of the buoy.

At Poole Fairway buoy the Decca will indicate the range and
bearing of the next waypoint (WPT2), which corresponds to
the change-over to the large scale chart 1106. If appropriate,
reset the cross track error (for NAVSTAR 2000D press WPT
WPT WPT 0 ENT). If tidal stream data has been entered,
then the course to steer displayed will compensate for this tidal
stream. Normally, for a passage over a period of twelve hours
the navigator will work out the course to steer allowing for the
tidal stream estimated for the whole leg of the passage – which
could mean that after six hours (the duration of one tide) the
cross track error might reach 15 nautical miles, though this will
be reduced as the tidal stream flows in the reverse direction. In
a motor boat travelling at a speed in excess of 10 knots (nautical
miles per hour) where the boat speed is significantly greater
than the rate of the tidal stream, the next waypoint can be kept
on a constant bearing using the cross track error facility.

The time of arrival at Poole Fairway buoy, and all sub-
sequent waypoints, should be recorded in the deck log together
with other relevant navigational data (distance log reading,
course to steer, engine hours, wind speed and direction,
barometric pressure). At regular intervals (every 30 minutes or
every hour on a longer passage) the time, distance log reading
and Decca position should be recorded in the deck log and the
position plotted on the chart.

On arrival at WPT2 the large scale chart should be used and

the tidal streams estimated for the rest of the passage to the harbour entrance so that the course to steer can be calculated by the navigator or by the Decca itself. There is no need to pass through the waypoint position as the Decca will normally indicate the closest point of approach and in some cases automatically switch the display to the next waypoint. If not, the display should be switched manually by selecting the next waypoint on the route and resetting the cross track error.

WPT3 is selected to be in the vicinity of CH1 landfall buoy off Cherbourg, but, more importantly, on the line or transit of the leading lights into the western entrance of Cherbourg harbour. From WPT3 to WPT4 the helmsman can keep on the transit line by using the Waypoint Cross Track Error display. He will be able to compensate automatically for the tidal streams which run across the approaches to the harbour.

ARRIVAL AT CHERBOURG

WPT5 and WPT6 enable the course to be set whilst landmarks within the harbour are identified. This can be quite important in poor visibility. Once secure in the marina, the Decca should be reprogrammed as necessary for Sailplan 2.

CHERBOURG TO ST VAAST-LA-HOUGUE

Because of the strong tidal streams and the possibility of rough seas off headlands, the passage from Cherbourg to St Vaast, though within sight of land all the way, requires careful planning to make best use of the tidal streams and to arrive at St Vaast within the period (2 hours 15 minutes before high water until 3 hours after high water) when the lock into the marina is operating. It is good navigational practice to mark alongside each waypoint the latest time of arrival (at the waypoint) to maintain a schedule to arrive at the destination at the optimum time (in this case the time of high water). It will then be readily seen whether the boat's speed needs to be increased (or whether a decision should be made to return to Cherbourg).

The procedure for the passage is much the same for that in Sailplan 1 but, as the tidal stream is likely to be along the boat's track rather than across, more use can be made of the *speed made good* and *estimated time to next waypoint* facilities.

9   Sailing to windward

TIDAL STREAMS

When plenty of navigation marks are visible, it is relatively easy for the helmsman to compensate for a cross tide (where the tidal stream is setting across the track of the boat). He would adjust the course into the tidal stream such that a near object, such as a buoy, remains in transit or in line with an object on the distant shore. The track would then be a straight line with automatic compensation for the sideways effect of the tidal stream. The buoy would remain on a steady bearing and the boat's course would correspond to the *course to steer*. If there was only one navigation mark visible, it would be necessary to use the hand-bearing compass to keep it on a steady bearing.

The same effect can be used with Decca when sailing or motoring to the next waypoint. The objective is to keep the bearing of that waypoint constant by periodic adjustments of the course steered. This is achieved in practice by keeping the *cross track error* down to a minimum. In this instance it is convenient for the helmsman to be able to see the Decca display. For most Deccas it is simple to reset the cross track error. For the NAVSTAR 2000D in the Waypoint Cross Track Error mode the cross track error is reset to zero by pressing `0 ENT`.

BEATING TO WINDWARD

When making a passage under sail it is frequently necessary to beat at 45° to the wind in order to reach the next waypoint. It is desirable to keep near to the direct track to the waypoint, if necessary choosing the tack (on which to beat) so that any tidal stream is pushing the boat towards the direct track. In the

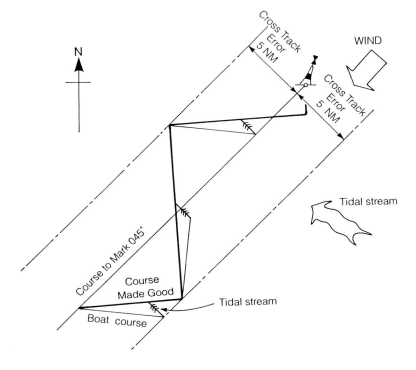

Fig 9.1   Beating to windward: the final approach should be with the tidal stream

Waypoint Cross Track Error mode, the boat should tack whenever the cross track error reaches (say) 5 nautical miles.

A better navigational technique for small boats is to draw on the chart a cone from the destination waypoint such that each side of the cone is 20° from the direct track from the start position. Measure on the chart the bearing of the waypoint along each side of the cone. The Waypoint Range and Bearing mode is then selected, with the boat tacking each time one of these bearings is reached such that the boat remains within the cone until the waypoint is close by.

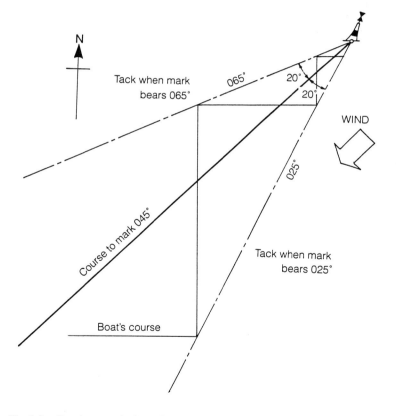

Fig 9.2   Beating to windward: remaining within a 40° cone

LAYLINES

When beating to windward, the layline is defined as the track that can be sailed to reach the next waypoint in the shortest possible time. The boat will tack when the layline is reached. The AP MK5 Decca, which accepts an input of wind direction, can calculate directly the time and distance to the layline. With other Deccas it is necessary for the navigator to note the course that can be steered on each tack and then draw the layline on the chart, allowing for any tidal stream. Using the course made good (from the Decca) from the present position, the point where this course intersects the layline can be plotted and the coordinates used as a subsidiary waypoint.

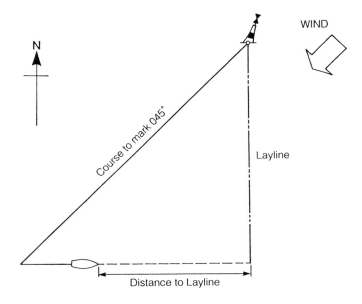

Fig 9.3   Beating to windward. Allowing for any tidal stream the layline is the optimum course (made good) for the mark. AP MK5 Decca calculates the time and distance to the layline on the basis of speed and course made good

10 Man overboard

When a crew member falls overboard, particularly at night, it is essential to record the 'man overboard' position so that the boat can return to the man in the water. Many Deccas allow for a 'man overboard' button to be installed within reach of the helmsman which, when pressed, will record the 'man overboard' position and switch the display to indicate the course and distance back to that position.

The full procedure in the event of a crew member falling overboard is for the helmsman or any other crew member on deck to:

1. Shout 'MAN OVERBOARD' to alert the rest of the crew.
2. Press Decca 'man overboard' button if near helmsman; or shout 'PRESS DECCA MAN OVERBOARD BUTTON' to the navigator.
3. Instruct a crew member to WATCH AND POINT CONTINUOUSLY TO THE MAN IN THE WATER.
4. Throw overboard lifebuoy (with light at night) and dan-buoy if carried.
5. Bearing in mind the state of the boat, of the sea and wind,

and of other craft in the vicinity, manoeuvre the boat, under power if possible, to return to the 'man overboard' position.

6. Recover the man overboard.

It is possible that the boat will have several sails set and it may take several minutes before the boat can be manoeuvred. The Decca will, however, indicate the course and distance back to the 'man overboard' position.

In the event of the boat being unable to return to the 'man overboard' position it will be necessary to alert the rescue services, giving them the latitude and longitude coordinates of that position and the time that the crew member fell overboard.

For those boats whose Decca is not fitted with a 'man overboard' button either remotely or on the set, then all crew members should be instructed on the key or button combinations to record the 'man overboard' position.

11 Operational limitations and accuracy

LIMITING RANGE AND COVERAGE

The different Decca chains vary to some extent in maximum range but typically this is about 250 nautical miles (460 kilometres) from the Master station by night and about 400 nautical miles (640 kilometres) by day.

During the night the ionosphere, which reflects the radio waves, becomes closer to the earth's surface and the skywaves, which are the reflected waves, interfere with the groundwave which is used by the Decca navigation system; see Fig 11.1.

Pages x and xi show the coverage of the Decca Navigator system around Europe. The shaded areas within the 'inner' limitation lines are those regions where the fix accuracy in daylight should be within 250 metres. The 'outer' limitation line indicates the range of effective operation, though Decca signals may be received and position displayed at considerably greater ranges in ideal conditions.

ACCURACY

Within the pattern of transmitter stations forming a Decca chain (see Chapter 14), the accuracy of a Decca position can be better than 50 metres. However, the transmission character-

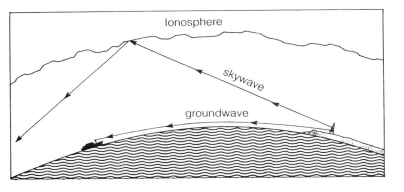

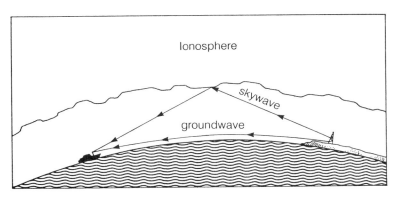

Fig 11.1   The effect of skywaves by day and night. By day (top diagram) the ionosphere is high and any reflected skywaves do not affect the signal received from the groundwave

By night (bottom diagram) the ionosphere is much lower and the reflected skywaves can interfere with the groundwave, causing considerable variation in signal strength

istics of the Decca signals are affected by coastlines (where the radio wave can be refracted) and by the time of day (signals are strongest at midday and weakest at midnight). There can be blanking of radio waves by high coastlines and industrial complexes, and deflection of radio waves when close to the masts of other yachts, such as in a marina.

Offset Position Correction

If a boat's position is accurately known and an error exists in the displayed position determined by the Decca signals, the difference between the two positions may be used to provide a fixed offset correction to all subsequently displayed positions.

This ability to apply an offset correction is convenient when returning to a regular mooring, but it can affect the accuracy of the indication of position at other geographical locations. If the boat's position is accurately known, and an error exists in the displayed position determined by the Decca receiver, the difference between the two positions may be used to provide a fixed correction to all subsequently displayed positions.

For the NAVSTAR 2000D position corrections are entered as follows: Press POS POS POS. Press ENT and +/− to freeze the display and select the position correction mode. Unfreeze the display, select the latitude scale and enter the correct latitude. Repeat to enter the correct longitude. When an offset position correction has been entered the indication of latitude in the display of present position is prefixed by the letter C.

12 Installation

Provided the instructions in the Decca receiver manual are followed, the installation is well within the capability of most boat owners.

MOUNTING POSITION

Most Decca receivers can be directly mounted in the cockpit area but it is usually preferable to mount the instrument in the navigation area of the cabin with a repeater on deck for the helmsman.

Those sets with liquid crystal displays (AP MK3, AP MK4, AP MK5, Shipmate) can be viewed to some extent in bright sunlight, but those with light emitting diodes (NAVSTAR, NASA) are best mounted within the cabin.

ANTENNA POSITION

The antenna may be mounted high up in an unobstructed position. With an appropriate bracket it can be mounted at the

Plate 2   Antenna installations

top of a mast but not where it is within 2 metres of the VHF antenna or in the signal path of a radar scanner. It can be mounted on the pushpit or, better still, on a two-metre metal tube clamped to the pushpit so that it is clear of any area of activity. On a motor boat it should be on the cabin roof as far as possible from other antennas. The antenna leads are either pre-wired or come with easily assembled connectors.

It is recommended that the structure to which the antenna is clamped be earthed via an earthing plate or anode.

POWER SUPPLY

The other important consideration is the power supply. Heavy currents (as needed for engine starting) can cause an alarming dip in battery voltage, which may cause the Decca to revert to its initialisation sequence. The use of twin batteries with isolator switches is helpful in this respect; and a separately switched direct connection from the receiver to a battery is worth consideration. The cable supplied is screened against interference but it should be kept well clear of engine alternators, dynamos, electric motors, windscreen wipers, fluorescent lights, pumps, winches and refrigerators. It is important that a good earth is provided for the screened cable; this should be via an earthing plate or anode and not via the engine or battery negative terminal.

The normal power consumption is just over half a watt. In sailing vessels contemplating passages in excess of 48 hours there will be a need for an auxiliary charging system, such as solar charging panels or wind generators.

A reception check that can be carried out after installation is for the boat to go out to sea well clear of other vessels and then proceed as follows:

1. Stop the engine.
2. Switch off all electrical equipment except the Decca.
3. Allow the Decca to complete its initialisation sequence and achieve signal lock.
4. Check the signal quality figures (see Chapter 6).
5. Start the engine, allowing it to run fast enough to charge the battery. Wait for 1 minute and recheck the signal quality figures. The figures should not change, but a drop of 1 unit in each figure is acceptable.
6. Repeat 5 above with engine in gear and motoring slowly.
7. Stop the engine and switch on all other pieces of electrical equipment one by one. Allow 1 minute for each item to warm up and then recheck the signal quality figures. A decrease of more than 1 unit may cause poor reception and thus affect the Decca accuracy. In such cases interference suppression should be fitted to the item concerned.

INTERFACING

Autopilot interfaces with Deccas enable the boat to be steered from waypoint to waypoint whilst fully compensating for tidal stream and any windage on the hull (leeway). There are usually built in to the Decca several types of interface, each with its own number such as NMEA 180, NMEA 181, NMEA 182 and NMEA 183. It is important that the interface used is compatible with that of the autopilot.

13   Types of Decca receiver

This chapter lists the types of Decca receiver available for small craft and gives a summary of the facilities available on each. Remember that for simple navigation many of the facilities will not be needed. The ways in which the facilities are used are discussed in later chapters.

AP NAVIGATOR

MK2 and 3 (no longer in production)
MK4 and 5

MK 2, 3 and 4 have also been marketed as Decca Yacht Navigator (DYN) MK 2, 3 and 4.

AP MK3

The AP MK3 Yacht Navigator was the first Decca receiver to become widely used in small craft. It is extremely versatile; though its operation is complex. *Yacht Navigator MK III –*

operation made easy, published by Mark One Publications International, gives full details of its operation.

AP MK4

The AP MK4 Yacht Navigator is small, yet it is easy to use and constantly displays precise information on position, course speed and steering. It has a good clear display, a compact, waterproof case and an excellent, easy-to-follow manual. With only a few buttons for its operation, the cursor has to be used to input waypoints; but with only nine waypoints this is not a disadvantage.

Plate 3   AP MK4 Yacht Navigator

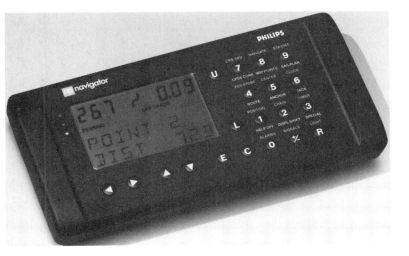

Plate 4   AP MK5 Yacht Navigator

AP MK5

The AP MK5 Yacht Navigator is a very sophisticated set offering many additional facilities, such as the calculation of true wind and tidal stream set and drift, time and distance to layline, and full interfacing with other electronic aids. It does require some time to be spent on operator training. The manual is large but easy to follow.

NAVSTAR

Model 603D (no longer in production)
Model 2000D

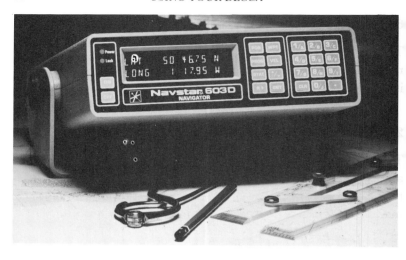

Plate 5   NAVSTAR 603D Mk II Navigator

Plate 6   NAVSTAR 2000D Navigator

603D Mk II

The NAVSTAR 603D Mk II Navigator is a very rugged and reliable receiver with full interfacing for other electronic aids. It is a little complex to use but easy enough with familiarity.

2000D

The NAVSTAR 2000D Navigator, with its separate normal and advanced modes, has comprehensive features and is easy to use. It has a superb set of quick-reference cards in place of a manual. Though performance in poor signal conditions is only average, it represents very good value.

Plate 7   NAVSTAR 2000D Combined Display Unit/Repeater

SHIPMATE

RS4500

The SHIPMATE RS4500 Navigation Centre (an updated version of the RS4100 Navigation Centre) is a very high technology device in which the Decca receiver is but a small part. It has a large gas-plasma display enabling a sketch chart to be drawn on which the boat's track will be recorded and updated using information from the integral Decca receiver or from the other instruments and electronic aids. In a simpler mode the digital read out gives position, course and speed made good, bearing and distance to next waypoint and crosstrack error. A very reliable, state-of-the-art electronic navigator marred only by the difficulty in reading the display in strong sunlight.

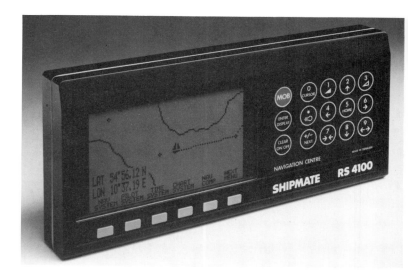

Plate 8   SHIPMATE RS4100 Navigation Centre

NASA MARINE

D200A

The NASA MARINE D200A Decca Receiver is a very simple navigator which only displays present position in latitude and longitude. The Decca chains have to be manually selected.

Plate 9   NASA MARINE D200A Decca Receiver

Others not generally available:

> WALKER
> LEAB
> VIGIL
> KELVIN HUGHES

Table 13.1 Decca Facilities

Compass deviation correction	Allows deviation of steering compass to be entered so that course to steer will be the compass course
Compass variation correction	Allows magnetic variation to be entered so that course and bearing can be displayed in magnetic terms
CPA warning	Alarm sounds at closest point of approach to waypoint
Datum selection	Different chart datums can be used (UK, Eire, Europe, Canada, S. Africa, Australia, Japan, India, Persian Gulf or WGS 72)
Dead reckoning computer	Computes position with manual entry of course, distance, etc.
Estimated position computer	Allows tidal data to be entered
Inter-waypoint data	Distance and bearing between any two waypoints
Keyboard lock	Keyboard can be disabled to prevent unauthorised alteration of data
Level of uncertainty	Display of predicted accuracy of fix (expressed in nautical miles)
Man overboard	When button is pushed, Decca will give course and bearing to return to the position where the 'man overboard' function was initiated

Manual chain selection	When in an area between two chains, Decca can be locked to one chain only to prevent discrepancies from successive readings being taken from a different chain
NMEA interface	Output/input for communication with other navigational instruments (speed log, compass, etc.) and autopilot
Position correction	If known position is different from Decca position then offset correction can be entered
Sail plans	Memorised routes consisting of waypoints in the order programmed in for that particular route
Timer	Timing device for racing starts, etc.
Waypoints	Maximum number of waypoints

Table 13.2 Comparison of Facilities

	AP MK3	AP MK4	AP MK5	NAVSTAR [603D]	NAVSTAR [2000D]	SHIPMATE [RS4500]	NASA [D200A]
Compass deviation correction					*	*	
Compass variation correction	*	*	*	*	*	*	
CPA warning	*		*	*	*	*	
Datum selection	*		*	*	*		
DR computer	*	*	*	*	*	*	
EP computer	*		*	*	*	*	
Inter-waypoint data		*		*	*	*	
Keyboard lock	*		*	*			
Level of uncertainty	*	*	*	*	*	*	
Man overboard	*	*	*	*	*	*	
Manual chain selection	*	*	*	*	*	*	*
NMEA interface	*		*	*		*	
Position correction	*	*	*	*	*	*	
No. of sailplans	10		10	1	9	9	
Timer	*		*	*	*	*	
No. of waypoints	10	9	200	25	99	200	0

14 Hyperbolic navigation

To understand how the Decca Navigator system works it is necessary to know something about radio theory. Radio waves are like sea waves with peaks and troughs. The distance between peaks or troughs determines the wavelength and hence, because radio waves travel at a constant speed, the frequency.

The frequency indicates how many peaks (or troughs) occur every second and is measured in cycles per second, usually known as Hertz (Hz). Radio frequences are measured in kilohertz (1kHz = 1,000 cycles per second) or megahertz (1MHz = 1,000,000 cycles per second). The Decca frequencies, in the range 70 to 130 kHz, are reckoned to be low-frequency signals.

When a receiver picks up signals at the same frequency from different transmitters they are said to be 'in-phase' if the peaks and troughs coincide and 'out-of-phase' if the peaks and troughs do not coincide. A receiver equidistant from two transmitters whose separate transmissions are in phase will receive the two signals in phase. If the receiver is nearer one transmitter than the other, the nearer transmissions will be

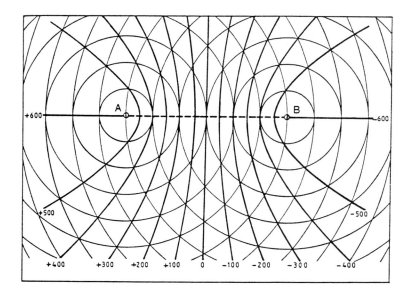

Fig 14.1   Construction of a hyperbolic pattern. The concentric circles
            represent the radio waves emanating from the transmitters A
            and B like ripples on a pond. The thick lines are drawn through
            the points of interaction where the difference between the
            distances to each transmitter is constant. These lines are defined
            as hyperbolae and are used by the Decca system as lines of
            position

received first, so the signals will be out of phase. The amount by
which they are out of phase will be proportional to the
difference in the distances from the two transmitters.

If a series of points are plotted for positions where the
difference in the distances of two transmitters is constant (i.e.
the phase difference is constant), then these points will form a
curve known as a hyperbola; see Fig 14.1. The Decca receiver
can measure the phase difference between the signals received
from a pair of transmitters and will thus know it is on the *line of
position* represented by the hyperbola for that phase difference.

The Decca Navigator system consists of a number of chains.
At the centre of each chain is a master transmitter, with two or

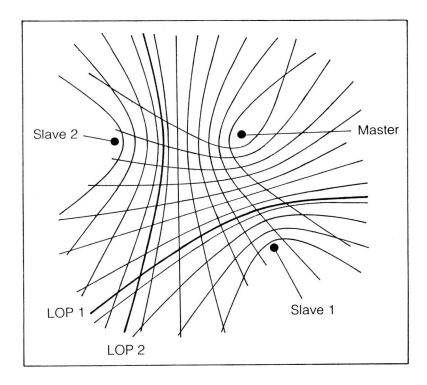

Fig 14.2   Hyperbolic lines of position

three slave transmitters some 50 to 150 miles away. Fig 14.2 shows a pattern of hyperbolae indicating distance (and hence phase) difference between a master and two slaves. Two lines of position have been plotted and where they intersect represents the position of the receiver. A fix can be obtained from two lines of position but a third line of position, from a third slave transmitter, improves the accuracy of the fix.

The Decca Navigator system is very accurate close to the transmitters where the *lattice* of the lines of position is compact; but accuracy drops off where the lattice opens out. The lattice is most elongated on the extended baseline from a master transmitter to a slave.

Appendix A   Elementary Navigation

As we have seen, it is quite simple to use your Decca in various ways without much prior navigational knowledge. In some ways it is all too simple: it is easy to rely entirely upon electronic aids to navigation without the back-up of the traditional well tried methods, bearing in mind that electronic aids can go wrong.

For this reason it is desirable to have sufficient knowledge to be able to keep, by basic plotting methods, a record of the boat's track and to estimate its position at a given time. Further, it is important to be able to check that position by taking bearings and plotting position lines to work out the course to steer from that position.

The basics of ESTIMATED POSITION, POSITION FIXING and COURSE TO STEER are given below, but for those who require further guidance the book *Day Skipper: Pilotage and Navigation* by the same authors and publisher is strongly recommended.

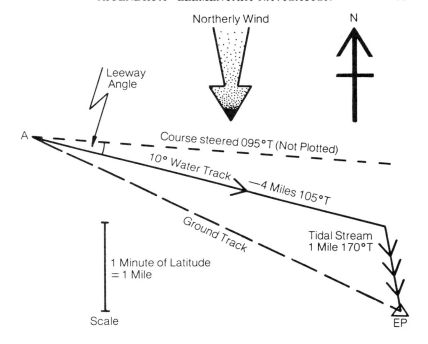

Fig A1   To determine an Estimated Position (EP), apply leeway and tidal stream to the boat's course steered

ESTIMATED POSITION

1. From the last known position (A), plot the water track (the track the boat is making through the water, having made allowance, if any, for the sideways drift caused by the wind).
2. Mark along the water track the distance the boat has travelled either by using the distance log or estimating it from the boat's speed.
3. Apply the tidal stream experienced during the period plotted.

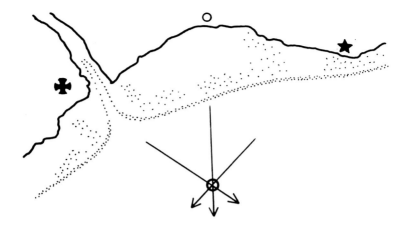

Fig A2   A plotted position fix from bearings on three objects. The
intersection is rarely so accurate as this

POSITION FIXING

1. Take bearings of visual objects with the hand bearing
   compass. At least two and preferably three bearings are
   required which give a good angle of cut.
2. Correct these bearings for variation (see later explanation).
3. Identify these visual objects on the chart and plot the
   bearings as position lines, making a note of the time.
4. The boat's position is where the position lines intersect.

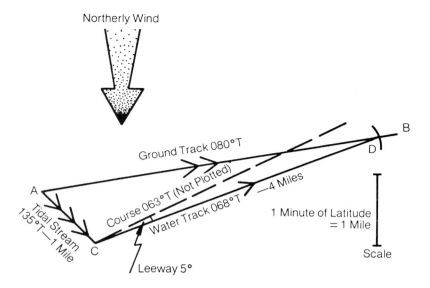

Fig A3   Finding the course to steer. To sail from A and B, this helmsman must initially steer 063°T. This brings him to point D after one hour, after which he must repeat the calculation, taking into account any changes in the tidal stream and leeway, for the remainder of the passage

COURSE TO STEER

1. From the position fix (A), plot a line representing the ground track to the destination (B) and measure the distance to go. Using the anticipated boat's speed, estimate how long it will take.
2. Again from the position fix, plot a line in the direction of the expected tidal stream (C) averaged over a period of one hour.
3. Using the dividers measure from the latitude scale a

distance corresponding to the boat's speed over a period of one hour (C).

4. Place one end of the dividers on the end of the tidal stream line (C) and mark the point at which the other end of the dividers reaches the ground track (D). This line is called the *water track* and it represents the direction that the boat must be steered to counteract the tidal stream.

5. Allow for any sideways drift (known as leeway) caused by the wind creating lateral pressure on the boat's hull. The course would be adjusted by steering towards the direction of the wind.

COORDINATES AND MEASUREMENTS

Latitude Scale

This is along the right and left hand borders of the chart. The divisions are degrees (°), minutes (') and tenths of a minute. Sixty minutes equals one degree. The divisions of the latitude scale are used as position coordinates and for distance measurement. One minute of latitude is equivalent to one nautical mile. Due to the way in which some charts are produced, it is necessary to measure distance on the latitude scale at the same level as the boat's position on the chart. See Fig 1.3.

Longitude Scale

This is along the top and bottom borders of the chart and the divisions are used as position coordinates. It is never used to measure distance. See Fig 1.3.

Compass Rose

See Fig 1.2. The compass rose consists of two concentric circles marked in degrees (°) from 0 to 360. It is used to indicate direction. The figure 0 on the outer circle corresponds with the direction of the true or geographic north pole and is known as True North. The figure 0 in the inner circle corresponds with the direction of the magnetic north pole and is known as Magnetic North. The meridians of longitude on the chart point towards true north but the needle on the magnetic hand-bearing and steering compasses are drawn towards magnetic north. The angular difference between true north and magnetic north is known as *variation*. The variation for the geographical location and its annual rate of change is written across the compass rose. Bearings taken with a hand-bearing compass will be magnetic so they need to be corrected before plotting on the chart as position lines. The magnetic material in a steel-hulled vessel can cause a further change in a compass reading. This change is known as *deviation* and has to be worked out for such a vessel by an expert compass adjuster.

Appendix B Glossary

Baseline extension

The extension of the line from the master transmitter station passing through the slave station. About 10 miles either side of this line Decca positions are suspect because of poor signal strength.

Chain

A group of Decca transmitter stations consisting of a master and three slaves, though there are some chains with only two slaves.

Chain change

In the area roughly equidistant between two chains the 'automatic chain selection' sometimes finds it difficult to correlate the positions obtained from the two chains and may indicate POSITION SUSPECT. It may be necessary to make the chain selection manually until clear of the doubtful area.

Chain selection

A manual facility for chain selection used to avoid problems with chain change areas.

Course made good (CMG)

The actual course followed by a boat under the influence of

tidal stream and leeway rather than its compass heading.

Course to steer
   The compass course steered by the helmsman. If appropriate
   it is converted to a true course by the application of variation
   and deviation.

Cross track error (CTE)
   The position of a boat relative to the track line between two
   waypoints expressed as a distance off to port or starboard of
   that track.

Dead reckoning (DR)
   The position determined from a fixed position using only the
   boat's speed and true course (through the water).

Deviation
   The error induced in a compass by shipborne magnetic
   influences.

Earthing plate
   A metal plate attached to the outside of the hull below water
   level to ensure a good earth connection for radio equipment.

Great circle (GC)
   The shortest distance between two points on the earth's
   surface. On a normal chart projection this may appear as a
   curved course. It is significant only for passages greater than
   200 nautical miles.

Heading
   The compass course (the apparent direction in which a boat
   is travelling).

Interface
   An electronic signal output suitable for operation in conjunction with other electronic aids or autopilots.

Lattice chart
   An Admiralty chart printed with a special overlay showing
   the lines of position radiated by Decca chains. Modern
   Deccas convert signals received directly into coordinates of
   latitude and longitude, making a lattice chart unnecessary.

Leeway

> The amount (expressed in degrees of angle) by which a boat is pushed off course laterally by the wind.

Line of position (LOP)

> A line used on a lattice chart to determine position.

Rhumb Line (RL)

> On a normal chart, the direct line between two points.

Speed made good (SMG).

> The actual speed made good by a boat over the ground (sea-bed), rather than through the water.

Track

> In the context of Decca navigation, the track is the direct line that a boat is following between two waypoints. The *ground track* is the course actually achieved by the boat over the ground (sea-bed); the *water track* is the course sailed through the water, making no allowance for tidal stream.

Variation

> The difference between the direction of true north and the direction of magnetic north. This varies with geographical position and is annotated on the compass rose on a chart.

Waypoint

> A point on a chart selected by the navigator either directly on a passage or as a reference point for alterations of course. The Decca receiver can be switched to indicate the range and bearing of any waypoint from the boat's present position.

Index

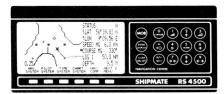